LANDSCAPE WITH SEX AND VIOLENCE

ALSO BY LYNN MELNICK

Please Excuse This Poem: 100 New Poets for the Next Generation, co-editor
(Viking, 2015)

If I Should Say I Have Hope
(YesYes Books, 2012)

POEMS
BY
LYNN
MELNICK

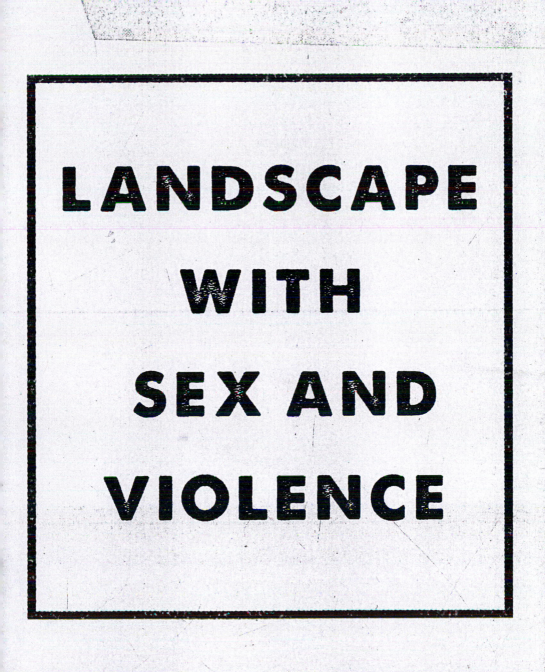

LANDSCAPE WITH SEX AND VIOLENCE © 2017 BY LYNN MELNICK

COVER ART: *TOPLESS DANCERS, FLORIDA 2003* © DAVID J. CAROL
PHOTO CREDIT: TIMOTHY DONNELLY
COVER & INTERIOR DESIGN: ALBAN FISCHER

FIRST EDITION, 2017
ISBN 978-1-936919-55-0

PRINTED IN THE UNITED STATES OF AMERICA

PUBLISHED BY YESYES BOOKS
1614 NE ALBERTA ST
PORTLAND, OR 97211
YESYESBOOKS.COM

KMA SULLIVAN, PUBLISHER
JILL KOLONGOWSKI, MANAGING EDITOR
STEVIE EDWARDS, SENIOR EDITOR, BOOK DEVELOPMENT
ALBAN FISCHER, GRAPHIC DESIGNER
BEYZA OZER, DEPUTY DIRECTOR OF SOCIAL MEDIA
AMBER RAMBHAROSE, CREATIVE DIRECTOR OF SOCIAL MEDIA
PHILLIP B. WILLIAMS, COEDITOR IN CHIEF, *VINYL*
AMIE ZIMMERMAN, EVENTS COORDINATOR
JOANN BALINGIT, ASSISTANT EDITOR
MARY CATHERINE CURLEY, ASSISTANT EDITOR
MARK DERKS, ASSISTANT EDITOR
COLE HILDEBRAND, ASSISTANT EDITOR
CARLY SCHWEPPE, ASSISTANT EDITOR, *VINYL*
HARI ZIYAD, ASSISTANT EDITOR, *VINYL*

FOR TIMOTHY DONNELLY

everything and always

"... there is no such thing as an innocent landscape."

—JARED FARMER

"Every time that I stare into the sun / Angel dust and my dress just comes undone"

—HOLE

CONTENTS

PART TWO

LANDSCAPE WITH SEX AND VIOLENCE

LANDSCAPE WITH STUCCO AND DANDELION

20th-century libertines peer from frosted glass
because they want to learn how I triumph, so

I am going to confess this once

    and then I am going to confess it again

in different ways I won't admit to but never mind.
This won't be the last time

    I let the riffraff envenom my body

while they pretend to be heroic.
This won't be the first time I faint against a building

where the weeds escape the cracks
into some kind of suffocating, mangled abandon.

Slumped against the sunlit stucco
I fail to keep my wits about me in a choke of triggers.

I down this dandelion poison because the promise
pitches a floral danger I could live inside.

I didn't emerge well-trained into this savage vista
because all the houseplants were succulent, and,

while anyone could witness rot writ all over my blighted arrangement,

no one stepped in.

PART ONE

LANDSCAPE WITH WONDER AND BLOWBACK

If I'm not a trinket I blend into concrete

so I rip my denim and bring enough musk to the car lot
to call it a cathouse.

The men are busy.
I stand quiet until they are busy

about me.

The bleak sun brightens on cement, sliding

into a feed ramp, no trigger guard
and you know how chatter happens

quickly among the gathering crowd.

    Dude, not a cloud in the sky!

Onlookers wonder how hard I fuck on gravel.

Hard:

I am the notched, cocking handle of any of your guns;
no one can safely touch me.

Everybody in my memory is young now.
Everybody in my memory is old though.

That's the blowback where my loose heart will fire.

LANDSCAPE WITH SMUT AND PAVEMENT

At night I hallucinate the grunting discord

which leapt from a human body as he destroyed mine.
That very month, I obliterated a beetle on a shiny walkway.

That month was November.

I think they are all out to get me,
all the insects in their armor.

Some folks like to use the word *slut*, even with children.

I am holding all my blood in vials on my lap.

The splatter is delicate.
I guess I am bleeding all over the scenery.

I was born in November.

But you want to hear about the clean stretch of pavement
where a beetle once lived

or the surrounding archways that were the kind of architecture
that bodies who have been treated gently like to enjoy.

The kempt lawn was always kempt.
I was disparaged on that terrain.

I was smut.
The rest was burnished.

LANDSCAPE WITH FANGS AND SEAWEED

To no one I said: *The dogs can't keep from staring.*
I said: *I have never been afraid of anything.*

    I forged a strut.

I lay on thick-grained sand
and fingered myself with chili on my tips

    to burn any thoughts under a foreign sky.

Meanwhile, he took the line of atrocity
all the way out to sea I could see through pearled glasses.

His wet skin wore the beach like scales
like scabies like the disease he was.

    He didn't allow me farther than the fence

so the strays stood guard while I showered
with my suit somewhere sunk

watching all those little boats in the distance
even though I knew

    to command salvation

would be impossible against the self-annihilation.
I said: *Yes, any man would have me over the seaweed*

   easy. I said: *Yes,*

all the wild dogs bare fangs.
I said: *Only one mouth claims my grit in its teeth.*

Say it's the '80s
and we're all wearing a whole lot of electric pink.

And I'm wearing it short.

I'm wearing it swimsuit, nowhere near the water.

I hire a skywriter to describe me:
voluptuous, terrified, bewitching, willing to wait

Somewhere in my schoolbooks it says to avoid
big crowds and flying objects

it says to check my work carefully
before the creep

with the grease-stained cuticles and menthol breath
does what he believes he was put in front of me to do

because
the skywriter got confused and wrote:

terrified, showstopping, mute, asking for it

No one in this town is surprised by the error,
they frown as I am always

pulling some sort of airshow
from the comfort of my crappy apartment.

But when the creep hits the field
to duck and cover

and the others scatter
with their hands over their visors over their eyes

and the plane crashes
headlong into the middle

of a more serious set of adjectives,
I'm pretty sure that the best solution here

is to get out of the '80s

and join the young Republicans pulling together
amid all the rubble.

LANDSCAPE WITH GREYHOUND AND GREASEWOOD

Mostly men keep singing
while dark blood collects where I open

and I line my polka dot panties with rest stop receipts.

I think probably we'll pause in Barstow to continue
these lyrics

but I'm no standard:

I fold over to smell myself.

Route 66 to Las Vegas.
Perfect for a child and also America

loves the promise of a long haul.

I pull the tab from a small can of apple juice:
see?

I'm cared for.
The man next to me puts his hand on my thigh.

He gets the kind of girl I am,
new leaves shiny with oil, flammable.

Come on.

Know better. Somebody,
know better.

LANDSCAPE WITH B-SIDE AND AIR HOCKEY

You'll be surprised
how firmly I can hustle a room full of players twice my age coming

off a pool table to the corner where I stand fondling quarters
waiting for someone to cut me

some slack because, the thing is, it's all defensive
play on a low friction surface

and I'm all instinct about a puck   *thin disguise*

If I tell you that a minor musician in the hall dubs me
a *clichéd-bit-of-flora-at-a-time-of-day-during-a-weather-event*

and later backs it with power chords—

well then!

Instant replay:
I stop the puck at the very last second

and knock it back so quick across the humming air
that my opponent pries a twenty from his billfold

and pulls me through the knot of bandmates to the back room where
jammed between two cabinets   *my one desire*

I endure my victory.

LANDSCAPE WITH CITRUS AND CENTURIES

Bodies clamber while the smudge burns and chokes
even some of our best guesses

so don't sink your teeth into the shrinking peel and call it victory
amid the downthrow.

Farmland and farmland and splendor and yet
I was never the type to wonder

what was sprouting from the fertile soil
when the soil itself was mystery enough.

Doomful orange garden!

Crop hangs over gates into dumpsters
though time was a girl could do anything with the right flora:

once, I used half a citrus to demonstrate
what you could do to my cunt.

I was born in what they call the heartland
but I've fretted the freehold length of California across centuries

enunciated through traffic groves
and whole orchards of dying fruit

hustling to raze each square of land
I will never call my own.

OBVIOUSLY, FOUL PLAY

I felt superior
on the other side of the door

when I still had hope about myself,
on the walk over, minding the traffic lights.

The flora.
The spiky city, neutral city

pushing me along from where I was
into what I knew to be wrong

(the other side of the door)
just to duck in, tuck under.

Some girls have their entire lives
ahead of them.

I used to imagine nothing

but hocus-pocus
would get me back

on my hands and knees
here in fancytown,

but this is not a crime scene
any of us can put into words.

In the champagne buckets,
spoiling milk.

In the champagne buckets,
years of surrender.

I don't so much give in as give up
in a room where the chandelier

has nothing of note to shine on
so it shines on me.

LANDSCAPE WITH LOANWORD AND SOLSTICE

Say yes
so I let him run me to the limits

in a pickup though I know better
than to expect

the chaparral
to grow much through trauma

except in order to withstand
extinction

though it appears
under the smog

supernatural.

CUT TO: he shoves my face
into the flatbed then punts me

when he's filled me.
Walk home and I do,

scrub for miles
the darkest day of the year moving in

and out of comprehension
but I am glad

(hear me? I am glad)
because now it can be over.

LANDSCAPE WITH LIMITLESS LANDSCAPES

Do you enjoy contradictions?
How about when my neck twists back at you and I wish I'd never laid

eyes on you, or I wish you'd keep your eyes to yourself

sometimes. Sometimes I need them.

The snake run looks a kick to carve
though I don't care for limitless landscapes; I need to be reined in.

Are you familiar with how one day can follow another?

At dusk you pick me up off the floor of the sidelines.

I'd like to think I could manage what other people do to me
even without this dust I'm snorting.

Lipstick palms loom to prove my point
and the way the dark hits the concrete, rounding it, undressing, well,

that too.

LANDSCAPE WITH WRITTEN STATEMENT

You wrap my ribs in gauze—
an experiment with the word *tenderly*

after your hands left my throat too bruised to speak.

While winter sun squints at the ghost flower
dying in its shabby terra cotta

far from home

men tell me to be honest about my role in the incident:

Okay, yes
I should have stayed inside

while you railed from the sidewalk

but my confused heart got into the car.

What happened is
I once spent too much time in the desert

so pogonip seems glamorous hung stuck in the trees
like when blood dries on skin

and I want to wear it

out for an evening,
pat my hands over its kinky path down my face

because: fuck you,

you didn't find me here.
I brought you here.

LANDSCAPE WITH SEX AND VIOLENCE

Consider this canvas of central valley splendor
    dull as the usual set of sucker punches—his distinctive

suggestion for a rainy day. I was crushed over sundry
    wonders of our topography.

Depraved though I was about my body
    I hated washing blood from my hair.

There is little I am good at.

I am good at sitting. That entire winter
    I sat outside in a town with too much earth

and I counted whorls slowly
    but I kept on with it, my pointless obsession, even though

I couldn't splay my sentences

damp into dark. I tried to detonate my body
    differently than he did. But then

came the sirens and then came the paperwork.

    Betrayed me: Hills of snails.

Behind me: How blood sticks to hair.

    Panorama: There is little I am good for.

LANDSCAPE WITH FOG AND FENCEPOST

I hear you in the kitchen
assembling soup from plastic

and kicking the cabinets again which is why
they're unsteady but what isn't and

it doesn't matter
you can't hammer a nail without drilling a hole through me first.

Left bare where you fastened me this morning
to the deck, faded to gray

inside the fogged air
muffling coastal California

I'm tied to the redwood of the fencepost
but I'm done with begging

naked
because this is only a blip in a lifetime of skin.

Cold, I bump up and try to think about things
other than cold

like how once you lit my hair on fire
and I watched it in the periphery

alight to my scalp
before I realized

I knew a way to stop it.

SHE'S GOING TO DO SOMETHING AMAZING

She's choking on the inspirational music
from the nurse tech's radio, something about running and fire

but like it's a good thing, like the fire is what drives all the running
and the running is toward something good and not from something

so violent

that when it catches her she ends up here
standing up slowly, blood still trickling down into her sock.

It's tinny, she realizes when she swipes a taste in the elevator

on her way out.

She passes each of the neat houses with red shingles
near the hospital in the posh part of town

and as she moves further away
the shingles take on an ashen color

the color of steak when it first starts
to move beyond bloody.

It's the color of the newly dying, is what she's trying to say.
It's the color of the world with all the bodies dying.

She'd meant to make a hook rug. Do you know those?
That's the kind of thing people did before computers

the kind of thing girls did before they were forced to suck dick
in the back of somebody's car.

The hook rug was of a reindeer, out of season,
and one of these seasons she had hoped

to be done with it and she'd lay it on her floor
like she'd been laid on the floor before and she'd lay on top of it

and she'd pull the threads out one by one
until her fingers burned and bled

and then she'd rage at herself for the ruin
and then she'd throw the whole ridiculous thing away

because whatever made her think she had any talent
for domesticity anyway.

There's an enduring chart on her.
When they need somebody with indefinable eyes

they call her up, they parade her around and inspect her.
They don't—what's the word—they don't

help her but they like to stand around
with their tongues down each other's throats

about how hot they are at rescuing girls.
Meanwhile, the blood keeps dripping down her legs.

She takes a job in a video store.
That's where people located porn before computers.

She watches men disappear
into the back room and she wants to tell them

she doesn't care what turns them on
but she wishes they wouldn't look crushed

when she won't touch their hands at the counter.
It's not the worst job;

it's just the kind of job you'd expect a girl like her to have.
But she doesn't care what you think.

She's going to get out of here eventually.
She's going to run triumphant circles around all you jerk-offs.

She's not bad at basketball, as long as nothing is flying at her face.
She likes the way asphalt smells like sweat smells like rubber.

That's the grace of being knocked nose-down,
that smell which is richer than skin

which suggests there once was victory even in this defeat.

Some nights at the discount laundry prove exciting.
This is where she finds herself with a scarf around her neck

holding a tissue just for effect. She's not crying anymore.
All her clothes look beige even when they are the colors she thought

would change her life into a life like other people might have
when they don't have blood dripping down their legs.

A stray gets into the building and everyone's got something to worry about
and everyone's a hero here because they are all so fucking concerned

about the dog, but she's taking her clothes
out of the dryer

and taking her scarf from around her neck and hanging herself
or hoping to

except she's too afraid of heights to climb higher than her height.
You maybe imagined her taller

when you picture her at night
when you imagine what holding her down was like—

more leggy, less bruised
about the thighs, about the throat, less hoarse.

She walks past the hospital where they long since took her chart
and used it to wipe between their legs

the hospital where no one remembers her
now that the worst thing

that ever happened to her happened
in the last century.

She stops bleeding.
Eventually, even metaphorically,

she stops bleeding.
She's going to go where no one knows they can't see her.

She's going to go where no one is getting high off her suffering
and then she'll be approximating a whole person

who may not play good basketball
and may not finish a rug in time for gift-giving

but wait, because she's waited.

She's going to do something amazing.

A man on a park bench wants to tell her a story.
It isn't what you're thinking.

He wants to tell her about the weeping willow that grew
in his boyhood backyard

in a different, easier land
and so she listens through his accent

and folds and unfolds herself on the bench

for most of the afternoon because his voice is gentle
and because it's the first time she's learned the name of a tree.

It's not that no one ever tried to teach her
it's that she couldn't understand

above the screaming.

LANDSCAPE WITH SURF AND SALVATION

Beachgoers frolic
   while I fuck a man shilling for Jesus

then cheer this collision
   of boredom and disconsolation

until their abandon leaves me pregnant. Imagine

all these suckering palms in pots of sand
   girding the clinic

like all the girls on gurneys awaiting their turn at pardon
   counting backwards

from twenty to tranquility.

Forgive anyone, I slur with wonder.
   Sketches of surf patch the ceiling

and I am sure I can hear gulls squawking toward heaven
   but it isn't salvation, just my own voice

coming to.
   If I'd have died I'd have scaled the fronds out of town

but I don't hemorrhage nearly enough
    to kill me just enough to feel

both of our bodies and the life leaving

both of our bodies.

LANDSCAPE WITH BLOOD AND BOONDOCKS

All the cats compass out at night to verify
my homelessness though you can't

expect me to claw for food while most everyone else is sleeping.
I'll just as soon not eat.

    I don't want anyone to keep me.

I'm a set of round, ridiculous things.
I talk claptrap in this lush

summer land of boondocks

(I thumb into somebody's car into somebody's car

and then we see if we can prove
every search for my body ends tragically)

and you point out a plume I don't care about

    over the rocks and ruffled around the blood I've lost.

I am thirteen before I know that ants can nest
in a log, fourteen before I know

that the reproductives have wings.

Under stag lights I dance for my dinner.
And everywhere I wander the cats scratch my legs.

I can't stay here. It's over, it was always over,
there was never going to be a miracle

that would keep me green.

PART TWO

LANDSCAPE WITH RUM AND IMPLOSION

You should have seen my breasts inside a dress so extravagant

it was rogue among a decade
of the type of electric horticulture

all these bittersweet groves were founded on so
yeah, I traded it right off my body

for a bottle of rum on the cleanest, brightest street corner
I didn't think to guard my skin against because

I'm in love with a woman who doesn't appeal to me.

Turn on the television and all you hear
is the new way of speaking

asked and answered

or the old new way of speaking now that everyone's doing it.

Am I happy about it? No.

I adapt to the manifold balconies of California
as a symbol of liberation

like the sophisticate I'm not
when no matter how many rails

we could finish from the railing
or the viewshed of a whole city against the neon of a floozy motel

I am only ever trapped inside

my own fixed vantage point or else I am
convention

imploding, such as it does.

POEM TO PROVE MY WICKEDNESS

I was just lying when you called
    the clangorous phone of this other

outskirt's motor lodge
    because of the places I'll put my tongue

that others won't.
    I'm no lady anywhere

and, like the sequoia that died
    girdled on display,

I'm older than I look.
    I've been double-dealing for a while now.

There's a reprieve in knowing
    where I belong and a world of ways

to prove myself disgraceful.
    Your fervency. Your remorse.

But all I had hoped for was that you'd
    convince me I'm more than just a body

while I moan *you can't leave*
    handprints on my throat.

DISTRESS CALL FROM THE CITY OF MY YOUTH

Punks tell me they have feelings
    while marching their crude revolution

toward my corner of Sunset, but I am worn
    out of feelings so I try again

to escape this lawless hunt

by fucking the archfiend dizzy on the backstreets
    because I don't understand how to deserve anything

or how misery and sunlight inhabit the same
    vibration in my skin.

Dear you, on the other end of the line:

I imagine how tenderly you'd peel the crime
    from what I left exposed

but my formative years were mostly alleyways
    and men being brutish so

I'm confused about a lot of things

like, I crossed this burning blacktop for you when
    I momentarily thought if I confessed

how long I've been open season, slaughtering season
    you might shoulder me past city limits alive.

YOU THINK IT'S TRAGIC BUT NO MAYBE NOT

In a life that's at least half over
    if I thought from the beginning

that few were looking out for me
    the horizon proves me right.

Only contrails in the sky. What if
    with no shadows I'm sneaking away?

What if I'm clothed? I want flight
    or I don't. I left for a spell, I left for

a spell and was cuffed and gagged
    and let go. I've never told anyone that.

A man in a clinic suggested I stop
    keeping secrets. So I'll share

with you my most recent fat lip, how
    the new red I bought covers it

pretty good. How it hurts when you
    kiss me and I don't dare look

up—there's no end to this—chemtrails,
    the world destroying itself.

POEM ENTERING THE APPLE VALLEY TARGET

Into the fluorescent rough country
headlong into bulks of flesh

impatient to outspend me

and who wouldn't fold real quick
under the weight of America's sales and specials.

I believed then I didn't

that I was different than I am
in my own skin in this infinity

mirror, instructed such
to seduce myself, to go on.

I am sorry

about the space I take up
about the panic

running around my aspect and my hunger

although it's nothing

these racks of acrylic winter apparatus
won't dazzle out of my head.

I'll take several. I'll take fistfuls.

I'll tuck it into my mouth at night to keep me quiet.

LANDSCAPE WITH TWELVE STEPS AND PROP FLORA

Inside that church in Hollywood
    you don't want to believe

what I'm about to tell you
    when you say I never speak when I say:

some boys take a beautiful girl
    and slam her against the wall.

Hey buddy, I didn't fight my way
    back from all the bruises and breaks

just to listen to you talk
    about my tits under string-lights.

I don't even know you. Sure, I do
    the most uncareful things

when I'm miles from here. It's all that
    freedom I don't recognize. But I have

nothing to say to you
    when you point out how far

you'd let me stumble in all the ways
    you listed down through

the netting in the plastic trees
    meant to protect the plastic trees

outside that church in Hollywood
    where the famous fuck-ups emerge

from the basement into a mob of cigarettes
    clouding up an already murky sky.

No, not like little stars, buddy.
    More like the end of the world.

POEM TO REMIND MY HEART TO BEAT

No matter the upright life I've been trying to lead
    I keep looking for new ways to bluff myself

so hard I'm always pleading for relief, frantically
    trying to locate whatever blunt object would sock me

into unconsciousness. I know what it's like
    to be powerless

on a shag rug. When I tell you—come closer,
    closer, look how pretty I am, come closer, close—

I will bury you there
    in this petri dish of what-went-wrong

growing in its dozens of gruesome sequences.
    It's October, slowly

the webs arch iron railings, the pumpkins appear
    like cautions, vigilant but motionless.

I would like that, my mood stabbed into me,
    triangle eyes blinking only the fire

behind them. Come closer, close; look how pretty
  I died on the shag rug, but you still

remember me. Autumn never did to me
  what it did to others, a beauty to admire

right before the end.
  I've been wrinkling, slowly, closer,

I need you to cuff me to whatever
  apparatus will pump the blood into

and out of my heart. Cut me open with chill-
  in-the-air, carve into me a face that can over-

take this unreasonable face. Closer, take me
  apart into your arms, I am not any brilliant color but

the dried brown leaf of the season folded over
  and stepped on by whatever step rushes

where any step is rushing to in all these crumbled pieces
  and in all these pieces I am sending myself

into the air to see where I land.

SOME IDEAS FOR EXISTING IN PUBLIC

I think you should grip your dick through your jeans and ask me

if I can handle it because you know I can, right?
I'm here for you.

I think you should overtake me at a bus bench
and invite me to sit on your face.

I think you should track me down
the block and clarify how you'd like to split my slit open

until I pass out.

(Once, as a kid, I was balancing on a ledge
all morning thinking no one

could see me until a man walked by and captured my chin in his grip
and called me *dollface*.)

I think you should screw me sideways right here on the sidewalk
like you said you might like to screw me

sideways before you took off
past the cop who said it's pointless to prove the crime so

come on, sure, screw me sideways, and why just sideways
why not all ways? Why not diagonal?

I think you should whistle so loud at my fat ass
that I jump like a stray rodent and you couldn't be more correct

it is a shame my fat ass is walking away

from you because why is it walking away from you?
Why am I walking away from you? Why am I here on the sidewalk?

I'm yours.

LANDSCAPE WITH THESAURUS AND AWE

There are 24 synonyms for the word *envy*.
And although one of them is *hatred* and one of them is *lusting*

no one envies me.

If I could just make it to morning without selling myself

one day I might have some land
beyond the ficus pot

whose heart leaves leak their poison
inside this slummy garage

where I sleep daytimes
in a city I'm sure I've mentioned before.

I am furious for answers
inside the book of words I stole from a stranger's back pocket.

You see, through the years when everyone is dying
I remain clean.

That's why I believe there could be a God.

There are 5 synonyms for the word *redemption*
and 46 for *fear*.

One of them is *chickenheartedness*
and another is *awe* and

only my body is for sale.

LANDSCAPE WITH SOMEWHERE ELSE NOW

No one walking here
will read my name into the road because I'm no one

and no one else would be walking here.
I don't penetrate a lot of sky although

if you believe the bulletin, I was sunshine.

Don't touch me. It's not strictly allowed.

Remember telephone wires?
The common raven never cared about me from up there

but I watched their carnage all down the coastline
and they watched mine behind all this thistle as the morning came up.

Somewhere else now

girls vibrate urgently for your tips and when I say girls

I mean that.

Biography ungags me
then saws the scene in half.

I'm ready. I've been my own excavator for years now
and it's always the same scree.

I instinctively touch my provocative hair.

POEM AT THE END OF A NEWS CYCLE

It wasn't until a gunman
landed in a parking lot in Kansas City

that I remembered how lucky I am
allowed to forget

there will be people who want to kill me
just for being Jewish, and

speaking of fortune
tonight I'm wondering if it's time to tell everyone

what it's like to panhandle Hollywood
for one lamp-heated burger or how quickly I could suck a cock

if cocaine wrapped up the transaction
and how, in the end, it really worked out okay.

This week everyone wants to talk about the California water wars
and my tongue

bathed in the metallic taste of the arch from the fountains
attached to all those cinder block hallways

I spent the latter years of the Cold War inside

although in those days it was something of a cinch
to get a flasket past security with my nipples as collateral

between the teeth of men with guns
who would otherwise fall asleep full of take-out

when they should have been guarding the wing.

So go ahead, draw me like a cartoon wimp
—*She's always having*

panic attacks, afraid of her own shadow—
more than once in my life

and I bruise kind of dark
but I've gotten to this point where I am just going to tell everyone

everything
that's ever been done to my face.

Last century the talk turned to the throng
out to see men unfurl a flag and flood

of riches upon Los Angeles
until all the rush killed a path on the way to the ocean

but you can watch me

save myself from harm with harm

so we celebrate
what is ruined but not dead and I've learned that

if there was an error in human judgment, I was the human
except I don't know what you would call this body

you're fucking.

So go ahead, draw me like a cartoon tramp—
Once a whore, always a whore, Lynn—

a plum shade of shame on my cheeks
because I've been impressed with such handiwork

since I first opened my legs

and I'll admit it, no problem:

I don't mind drawing and my skill is almost passable
but I'm not gonna work for free.

On Fountain there was a girl who'd groan my name how she said it
would sound in Spanish

while I bit her along the downslope
winds waiting for men and then men

swept us off the street

though she alone was handcuffed in a cell
while a man with a gun brought me a Coke in the waiting room

and real quick I understood enough about bigotry and drought
to swallow it all

without lifting my lids at either of them.

Last year everyone wanted to talk about gun violence
and how America was founded on a certain measure of blood

which isn't a metaphor nor was it
anywhere in California

in the back of a car when a man asked

'bout I ram this barrel up your pussy and pull the trigger?

but I wish at present we could talk about the environment
a little bit

like the cranesbill on the side of the road
I pled my way down

to propagate easily in the absence of rain.

This week everyone wants to talk about sex work
but I don't

want to hear about how it's just like waitressing
or the time I watched a friend fold shirts at a boutique

though, true, the rigor and relentlessness
made me tight in the chest and the slightest bit exhilarated

the way I feel following down that whole list of things
I'm surprised to have the skillset for

but if there hasn't been a moment at your job
where for an extra $10 you let a man spit on your face

and cum in your eye

then I don't want to hear about all the empowerment

I failed to find.

LANDSCAPE WITH DISSOCIATION

Come love,
let's observe this brouhaha

form in an unskilled meter about the blood
trail up and down the noted coast

and, with so many faces
needing more and more of what I am: kaput

hot-to-trot

through the courtyards and, dear god, the greenery,
well, these days I feel the need to muck things up a bit

just so I recognize myself.

I rode out the bullish '80s under textured plaster
so I know a crime when I commit one

and I know you know I would bang my own mouth
if it might muzzle my watchfulness

but how about we keep this clean.

I go hunting for another word for *hypervilgilance*
and someone asks if I mean *hopefulness*.

I do not.
But whatever.

I guess I'll just stand here now
and read to you about any of the times I managed to live

when it sure is a roughhouse, isn't it,

living.

I was warned more about rattlesnakes
than anything I actually lived with

(they rarely bite)

so I memorized the diagram
imagined running, knew intimately

the gruesome belt snap before leather hit my skin

couldn't stop who could

welt me

and, oh, that?
that's just a pit viper, spell it, venom, spill it—

look,
we played in alleys and it was good, clean fun and

sure,
someone had a yard (affection, branches, not mine)

with a wooden swing but I got so scared up there
I accidently pissed on it

(dishonor, dismay)
no wonder

I'm back counting empties
lining them up for the boys to bowl

(tarmac, blacktop, lonesome)

LANDSCAPE WITH PINWEED AND STUNT DOUBLE

Across the alleyway from myself there I am
lit by Hollywood in a decalescent dress

which feels just by looking at it

that someone's holding my hips and going at me face down

but I've seen my ringer in a stern scarf throw
her keys at would-be punks

and catch one at the back of the head so hard he called up a loud
"goddamn it, bitch!" and I envied that

as I never really learned how to finish an interaction
without letting semen inside me somewhere.

To the Woman Across the Alleyway:

the worst thing of all
was pretending

it wasn't happening or maybe in that moment I convinced myself
it was happening to someone else.

Living in this wasteland
I didn't wear a scarf until I was too old to risk

anything around my neck

and would just as soon
groan into a chokehold than wear it

as fashion though grubs have fed on me in every season
because I'm a lush

tacky annual unwinding in rare humidity toward self-burial
or, I mean

once I pull my true self from the split.

LANDSCAPE WITH HAPPILY EVER AFTER

Near midnight I'm held
hostage to the hazy upshot in the corner

velvet near a laced up tree and curious how I got here.

What a crowd! I think
and I think I should hoard my stash in my shoe.

Did you catch the census takers trying to autocorrect
the shelterbelt out of my history

when meanwhile

I've been fending off elements
since I first showed up at this latitude so

I don't trust easy.

In 5, 4, 3, 2, 1
you ask me outside

where the music dims
against the complicated bramble

and I love how the moon

is gilding the rusted basketball hoop in the driveway
and bouncing off the sheen of the rubber tree

and onto this fable
in a city that bleeds its saline soil

into another difficult year.

LANDSCAPE WITH CLINIC AND ORACLE

Maybe you're not the featherweight champ
of all the cutthroat combat sports

(fifteen and pregnant
again)

but you'd convert your ring corner
into a slaughterhouse

before you'd inquire after human kindness.

In the humdrum flare outside the clinic
you wait for a ride, feel the spill at the tipping point

trickle down your inner thigh
as you bask in the post-industrial particulate

on your skin, ash
into a jasmine pot's bituminous anchorage

so tacky it glows in a habitat that spent your body
long before it finished growing.

Lynn! they lied to you

don't you know?
Your womb will be the first thing to heal.

What you smell is pleasure, not the rot of the thing
amid the waste.

You will have babies.
You will write poems about flowers that turn on in darkness.

ONE SENTENCE ABOUT LOS ANGELES

I've been trying to plant a palm in every garden
I slink through

using this intoxicating body I lucked into
some years after I first arrived

in the desert in a Datsun
with a commonplace finch in the back bench seat with me

and, while you're probably waiting for metaphors
because you know that's the most respectable skill I have

this is not a story about cages
and it sure isn't a story about wings

and, while you are probably waiting for confession
because you think that's what I've been doing here all along

this is not a story of how my body was first held down
before I'd even hit double digits

on a dingy carpet whose fibers are still
on my tongue, whose burn to my cheek I didn't even notice

amid the more traumatic injuries

until later I saw photos
because I couldn't look in the mirror

until the 21st century
but this, all of this, the rape and the allegory

and the skinny palms sheltering no one:

this is the story of how I got to live

in a city that had run one course and needed
another, roots humping

up the walkways so even sober we stumbled
toward the slowing cars which is what happens to girls

who grow up with all that poetry and carpet
in their mouths but remember

(I almost forgot to tell you)

I lived

in a desert
where palms are signposts of water, not the want of it.

The first epigraph is taken from Jared Farmer's book *Trees in Paradise: A California History*. I owe a huge debt of gratitude to this book for its wealth of information and inspiration.

The second epigraph is taken from the song "Asking for It," written by Courtney Love and Eric Erlandson, and performed by Hole.

"Landscape with Wonder and Blowback," "Landscape with Limitless Landscapes," and "You Think It's Tragic But No Maybe Not" were written after Ashly Stohl's photographs, "James Quaintance, 2011," "James Quaintance, 2011," and "Venice Beach, California, 2010."

"Landscape with Rum and Implosion" includes a slightly altered phrase from the song, "Things Have Changed," written and performed by Bob Dylan.

"Landscape with Twelve Steps and Prop Flora" includes a phrase from the song, "Girls Just Wanna Have Fun," written by Robert Hazard and performed by Cyndi Lauper.

"Poem to Remind My Heart to Beat" takes its title from a line in Emily Brontë's *Wuthering Heights*: "I have to remind myself to breathe—almost to remind my heart to beat!"

"Landscape with Thesaurus and Awe" owes a debt to Melissa Broder, who asked me to write about envy.

"Landscape with Somewhere Else Now" was written after David J. Carol's photograph entitled "Topless Dancers, Florida 2003." (This is also the cover photo.)

In "Poem at the End of a News Cycle," the line "If there was an error in human judgment, I was the human" was inspired by the testimony of William Mulholland during the Los Angeles Coroner's inquest into the deadly St. Francis Dam collapse of 1928.

"Green and Golden" takes its title from the poem "Fern Hill" by Dylan Thomas, which is, to the best of my memory, the first poem I ever read.

"Landscape with Pinweed and Stunt Double" includes lines from an interview that Courtney Love gave for a *New York Magazine* article, entitled "Feminism, Amplified," on June 3, 1996. The lines used refer to the impetus behind the song "Asking for It."

With heartfelt gratitude to the following publications, in which these poems first appeared, and to their editors and readers, whose support has been crucial:

Academy of American Poets' Poem-a-Day, APR, The Awl, Chicago Quarterly Review, Good Men Project, Gulf Coast, Dusie, Eleven Eleven, Epiphany, The Journal, Manhattanville Review, New Republic, The New Yorker, The Offing, Omniverse, Phantom Books, Prairie Schooner, Public Pool, A Public Space, Smoking Glue Gun, TheThe Poetry, Two Peach, VERSE, Vinyl, and *Washington Square Review*

"Landscape with Smut and Pavement," "Some Ideas for Existing in Public," and "One Sentence About Los Angeles" appear in the anthology *A Shadow Map* (Civil Coping Mechanisms, 2017)

"Landscape with Rum and Implosion" appears in the anthology *Brooklyn Poets Anthology* (Brooklyn Arts Press, 2017)

"You Think It's Tragic But No Maybe Not" appears in the anthology *Among Margins: Critical & Lyrical Writing on Aesthetics* (Ricochet Editions, 2016)

"Some Ideas for Existing in Public" appears in the anthology *Bettering American Poetry 2015* (Bettering Books, 2016)

"Landscape with Somewhere Else Now" appears in the anthology *Political Punch* (Sundress Publications, 2016)

"Landscape with Written Statement," "Landscape with Sex and Violence," "Landscape with Pinweed and Stunt Double," "Landscape with Blood and Boondocks," and "Landscape with Rum and Implosion" were translated into Spanish and published in *Circulo de Poesia* (Mexico)

"Landscape with Blood and Boondocks" was translated into Dutch and published in *OoteOote* (Netherlands)

"Landscape with Stucco and Dandelion" was made into a broadside by Fort Gondo Art Center, St. Louis, MO

"Landscape with Wonder and Blowback," "Landscape with Limitless Landscapes," and "You Think It's Tragic But No Maybe Not" were made into broadsides by Vela Noche and the Poetry Society of America, NYC

"Landscape with Blood and Boondocks" was made into a broadside by the Center for Book Arts, NYC

*

I am enormously lucky and grateful to receive so much love from friends and family. *It does not go unnoticed.*

For their advice, fortitude, and care during the writing of this book, thank you to Mary Jo Bang, Mark Bibbins, Rachel Boynton, Kelly Forsythe, Brianne Johnson, Brett Fletcher Lauer, Ricardo Maldonado, Ashly Stohl, and Barbara White. To the Brooklyn Po-Moms and to the Binder Poets.

To Anita and Michael Melnick, and to Cliff and Jessica Melnick, with love always.

To all of my VIDAs. Especially to Amy King, Camille Rankine, Hafizah Geter, and Melissa Febos. I am every day lifted by your work, your humor, your bravery, and your compassion.

To Jess Workman, who was there, and to Kimmy Lopez, wherever she is. And to the late Phil Bosakowski.

Huge thank yous to KMA Sullivan, editor and friend, to Alban Fischer and Jill Kolongowski, and to the whole YesYes Books team. Also huge gratitude to David J. Carol for his generosity with the cover photograph.

Deep respect and support always to victims of violence, harassment, and patriarchy. I hear you and I believe you.

Thank you endlessly to Timothy Donnelly and to Ada and Stella Donnelly. You make every landscape extraordinary. I love you.

FULL-LENGTH COLLECTIONS

i be, but i ain't by Aziza Barnes

The Feeder by Jennifer Jackson Berry

Love the Stranger by Jay Deshpande

Blues Triumphant by Jonterri Gadson

North of Order by Nicholas Gulig

Meet Me Here at Dawn by Sophie Klahr

I Don't Mind If You're Feeling Alone by Thomas Patrick Levy

If I Should Say I Have Hope by Lynn Melnick

some planet by jamie mortara

Boyishly by Tanya Olson

Pelican by Emily O'Neill

The Youngest Butcher in Illinois by Robert Ostrom

A New Language for Falling Out of Love by Meghan Privitello

I'm So Fine: A List of Famous Men & What I Had On by Khadijah Queen

American Barricade by Danniel Schoonebeek

The Anatomist by Taryn Schwilling

Gilt by Raena Shirali

Panic Attack, USA by Nate Slawson

[insert] boy by Danez Smith

The Bones of Us by J. Bradley

    [Art by Adam Scott Mazer]

CHAPBOOK COLLECTIONS

VINYL 45S
After by Fatimah Asghar
Inside My Electric City by Caylin Capra-Thomas
Dream with a Glass Chamber by Aricka Foreman
Pepper Girl by Jonterri Gadson
Of Darkness and Tumbling by Mónica Gomery
Bad Star by Rebecca Hazelton
Makeshift Cathedral by Peter LaBerge
Still, the Shore by Keith Leonard
Please Don't Leave Me Scarlett Johansson by Thomas Patrick Levy
Juned by Jenn Marie Nunes
A History of Flamboyance by Justin Phillip Reed
No by Ocean Vuong

BLUE NOTE EDITIONS
Beastgirl & Other Origin Myths by Elizabeth Acevedo

COMPANION SERIES
Inadequate Grave by Brandon Courtney
The Rest of the Body by Jay Deshpande